Look What I Can Color!

out and about

Dear Parents and Caregivers,

Welcome to Look What I Can Color!—a new style of coloring and activity book series for prekindergarten and kindergarten children. Each 256-page book includes fun, bold, and easy-to-color pictures.

The activities in this book support the following skills:

- color recognition
- number recognition
- visual processing
- tracing
- coloring
- matching
- fine motor skills

To find other educational products to help your child learn and grow, look for the ⊙ logo and visit **www.carsondellosa.com** or your local bookseller.

Sincerely,

Your friends at Rainbow Bridge

Color the picture.

Follow the number key to color the picture.

1 2 3 4 5 6

Trace the colored lines to finish the picture.

Color the big picture to match
the little picture.

Color the picture.

Follow the number key to color the picture.

Trace the colored lines to finish the picture.

Color the big picture to match
the little picture.

Color the picture.

Follow the number key to color the picture.

Trace the colored lines to
finish the picture.

Color the big picture to match
the little picture.

Color the picture.

Follow the number key to color the picture.

1 2 3 4 5 6

Trace the colored lines to
finish the picture.

Color the big picture to match the little picture.

Color the picture.

Follow the number key to color the picture.

1   2   3   4   5   6

Trace the colored lines to
finish the picture.

Color the big picture to match
the little picture.

Color the picture.

Follow the number key to color the picture.

Trace the colored lines to finish the picture.

Color the big picture to match
the little picture.

Color the picture.

Follow the number key to color the picture.

(1) (2) (3) (4) (5) (6)

Trace the colored lines to
finish the picture.

Color the big picture to match
the little picture.

Color the picture.

Follow the number key to color the picture.

1 2 3 4 5 6

Trace the colored lines to
finish the picture.

Color the big picture to match
the little picture.

Color the picture.

Follow the number key to color the picture.

Trace the colored lines to
finish the picture.

Color the big picture to match
the little picture.

Color the picture.

Follow the number key to color the picture.

1 2 3 4 5 6

Trace the colored lines to
finish the picture.

Color the big picture to match the little picture.

Color the picture.

Follow the number key to color the picture.

1 **2** **3** **4** **5** **6**

Trace the colored lines to
finish the picture.

Color the big picture to match
the little picture.

Color the picture.

Follow the number key to color the picture.

(1) (2) (3) (4) (5) (6)

Trace the colored lines to
finish the picture.

Color the big picture to match
the little picture.

Color the picture.

Follow the number key to color the picture.

1 2 3 4 5 6

Trace the colored lines to finish the picture.

Color the big picture to match
the little picture.

Color the picture.

Follow the number key to color the picture.

Trace the colored lines to
finish the picture.

Color the big picture to match
the little picture.

Color the picture.

Follow the number key to color the picture.

1 2 3 4 5 6

Trace the colored lines to
finish the picture.

Color the big picture to match
the little picture.

Color the picture.

Follow the number key to color the picture.

(1) (2) (3) (4) (5) (6)

Trace the colored lines to
finish the picture.

Color the big picture to match the little picture.

Color the picture.

Follow the number key to color the picture.

Trace the colored lines to finish the picture.

Color the big picture to match
the little picture.

Color the picture.

Follow the number key to color the picture.

Trace the colored lines to
finish the picture.

Color the big picture to match
the little picture.

Color the picture.

Follow the number key to color the picture.

1 2 3 4 5 6

Trace the colored lines to
finish the picture.

Color the big picture to match
the little picture.

Color the picture.

Follow the number key to color the picture.

Trace the colored lines to
finish the picture.

**Color the big picture to match
the little picture.**

Color the picture.

Follow the number key to color the picture.

1 2 3 4 5 6

Trace the colored lines to
finish the picture.

Color the big picture to match
the little picture.

Color the picture.

Follow the number key to color the picture.

Trace the colored lines to finish the picture.

Color the big picture to match the little picture.

Color the picture.

Follow the number key to color the picture.

1 2 3 4 5 6

Trace the colored lines to
finish the picture.

Color the big picture to match
the little picture.

Color the picture.

Follow the number key to color the picture.

Trace the colored lines to
finish the picture.

Color the big picture to match
the little picture.

Color the picture.

Follow the number key to color the picture.

1 2 3 4 5 6

Trace the colored lines to finish the picture.

Color the big picture to match the little picture.

Color the picture.

Follow the number key to color the picture.

1 2 3 4 5 6

Trace the colored lines to finish the picture.

Color the big picture to match
the little picture.

Color the picture.

Follow the number key to color the picture.

1 2 3 4 5 6

Trace the colored lines to
finish the picture.

Color the big picture to match the little picture.

Color the picture.

Follow the number key to color the picture.

1 2 3 4 5 6

Trace the colored lines to
finish the picture.

Color the big picture to match
the little picture.

Color the picture.

Follow the number key to color the picture.

1 2 3 4 5 6

Trace the colored lines to
finish the picture.

Color the big picture to match
the little picture.

Color the picture.

Follow the number key to color the picture.

(1) (2) (3) (4) (5) (6)

Trace the colored lines to
finish the picture.

Color the big picture to match
the little picture.

Color the picture.

Follow the number key to color the picture.

1 2 3 4 5 6

Trace the colored lines to
finish the picture.

Color the big picture to match
the little picture.

Color the picture.

Follow the number key to color the picture.

1 2 3 4 5 6

Trace the colored lines to
finish the picture.

**Color the big picture to match
the little picture.**

Color the picture.

Follow the number key to color the picture.

Trace the colored lines to
finish the picture.

Color the big picture to match
the little picture.

Color the picture.

Follow the number key to color the picture.

(1) (2) (3) (4) (5) (6)

Trace the colored lines to
finish the picture.

Color the big picture to match the little picture.

Color the picture.

Follow the number key to color the picture.

Trace the colored lines to finish the picture.

Color the big picture to match
the little picture.

Color the picture.

Follow the number key to color the picture.

Trace the colored lines to
finish the picture.

Color the big picture to match
the little picture.

Color the picture.

Follow the number key to color the picture.

1 2 3 4 5 6

Trace the colored lines to
finish the picture.

Color the big picture to match
the little picture.

Color the picture.

Follow the number key to color the picture.

(1) (2) (3) (4) (5) (6)

Trace the colored lines to finish the picture.

Color the big picture to match the little picture.

Color the picture.

Follow the number key to color the picture.

1 2 3 4 5 6

Trace the colored lines to
finish the picture.

Color the big picture to match the little picture.

Color the picture.

Follow the number key to color the picture.

1 2 3 4 5 6

Trace the colored lines to
finish the picture.

Color the big picture to match
the little picture.

Color the picture.

Follow the number key to color the picture.

1 2 3 4 5 6

Trace the colored lines to finish the picture.

Color the big picture to match
the little picture.

Color the picture.

Follow the number key to color the picture.

1 2 3 4 5 6

Trace the colored lines to
finish the picture.

**Color the big picture to match
the little picture.**

Color the picture.

Follow the number key to color the picture.

Trace the colored lines to finish the picture.

Color the big picture to match
the little picture.

Color the picture.

Follow the number key to color the picture.

1 2 3 4 5 6

Trace the colored lines to
finish the picture.

Color the big picture to match
the little picture.

Color the picture.

Follow the number key to color the picture.

1 2 3 4 5 6

Trace the colored lines to finish the picture.

Color the big picture to match
the little picture.

Color the picture.

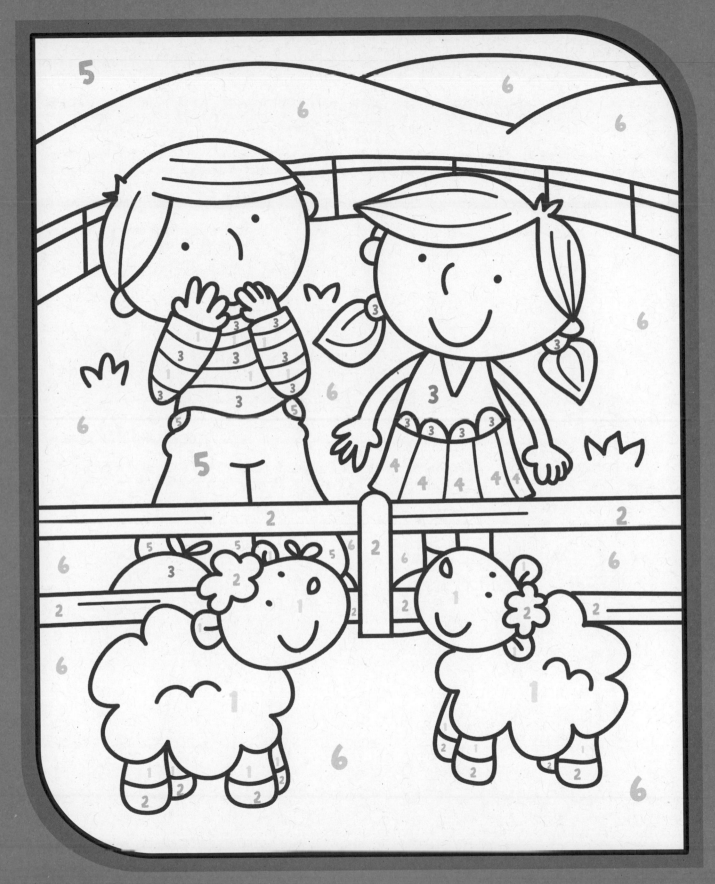

Follow the number key to color the picture.

(1) (2) (3) (4) (5) (6)

Trace the colored lines to
finish the picture.

Color the big picture to match the little picture.

Color the picture.

Follow the number key to color the picture.

Trace the colored lines to
finish the picture.

Color the big picture to match
the little picture.

Color the picture.

Follow the number key to color the picture.

① ② ③ ④ ⑤ ⑥

Trace the colored lines to
finish the picture.

Color the big picture to match
the little picture.

Color the picture.

Follow the number key to color the picture.

1   2   3   4   5   6

Trace the colored lines to
finish the picture.

Color the big picture to match the little picture.

Color the picture.

Follow the number key to color the picture.

Trace the colored lines to
finish the picture.

Color the big picture to match
the little picture.

Color the picture.

Follow the number key to color the picture.

1 2 3 4 5 6

Trace the colored lines to
finish the picture.

Color the big picture to match the little picture.

Color the picture.

Follow the number key to color the picture.

(1) (2) (3) (4) (5) (6)

Trace the colored lines to
finish the picture.

Color the big picture to match
the little picture.

Color the picture.

Follow the number key to color the picture.

1 2 3 4 5 6

Trace the colored lines to
finish the picture.

Color the big picture to match the little picture.

Color the picture.

Follow the number key to color the picture.

(1) (2) (3) (4) (5) (6)

Trace the colored lines to
finish the picture.

Color the big picture to match
the little picture.

Color the picture.

Follow the number key to color the picture.

1 2 3 4 5 6

Trace the colored lines to
finish the picture.

Color the big picture to match
the little picture.

Color the picture.

Follow the number key to color the picture.

Trace the colored lines to
finish the picture.

Color the big picture to match
the little picture.

Color the picture.

Follow the number key to color the picture.

(1) (2) (3) (4) (5) (6)

Trace the colored lines to
finish the picture.

Color the big picture to match
the little picture.

Color the picture.

Follow the number key to color the picture.

Trace the colored lines to
finish the picture.

Color the big picture to match the little picture.

Color the picture.

Follow the number key to color the picture.

1   2   3   4   5   6

Trace the colored lines to
finish the picture.

Color the big picture to match the little picture.

Color the picture.

Follow the number key to color the picture.

1   2   3   4   5   6

Trace the colored lines to
finish the picture.

Color the big picture to match the little picture.

Color the picture.

Follow the number key to color the picture.

1 2 3 4 5 6

Trace the colored lines to finish the picture.

Color the big picture to match
the little picture.

Color the picture.

Follow the number key to color the picture.

(1)   (2)   (3)   (4)   (5)   (6)

Trace the colored lines to finish the picture.

Color the big picture to match
the little picture.

Color the picture.

Follow the number key to color the picture.

1 2 3 4 5 6

Trace the colored lines to
finish the picture.

Color the big picture to match
the little picture.

Color the picture.

Follow the number key to color the picture.

1 2 3 4 5 6

Trace the colored lines to
finish the picture.